The Practice of
Facilitative Leadership

Ken Todd Williams

Introduction

There are so many published works on leadership one could conclude there is no other topic so mysterious or complex (other than love or happiness). There are dozens of schools of thought about the nature and promise of leadership and thousands of programs, books, and seminars.

We can get some hint of the diversity of viewpoints on leadership by walking through the business section of a major bookstore. So many titles on leadership include an adjective which serves to position or anchor the author's framework, an adjective such as "charismatic," "adaptive," "connective," "collective," "primal," "servant," or "transformational." It takes a deep dive into these books to determine whether something revolutionary is being said about leadership or whether there is just a rehash of existing ideas.

Some people, particularly emerging social justice leaders, have argued that it is time to abandon the social construct of "leadership" altogether. These are individuals who have suffered and survived at the mercy of self-serving hierarchies or observed others doing so. Such free thinkers argue that a fixed, position-based notion of leadership is antiquated, inherently divisive, and alienating. These advocates would prefer to see leadership described as a *process* rather than a *status* or jettisoned as a term of trade altogether in favor of emphasis on and recognition for the living, loving works of collectives.

In practice, however, it is extremely difficult, if not impossible, to eliminate the powerful idea of "individuated" leadership which includes personal contributions, role modeling, and impactful acts of facilitation or service ("interventions"). What is needed in most endeavors is not an abandonment of the construct of leadership, but rather a collective purging of harmful behaviors and broad-based adoption of habits embedded in empathy. Leadership must be rehabilitated in some contexts and readily distinguished from dominance, entitlement, and indifference.

Substantial work remains to be completed in the construction of a leadership theory that can be *easily applied*. To be well led, our institutions and communities do not need a list of leaders' traits. What most groups need today, in addition to ample resources, are clear, straightforward frameworks, captured in principles, stories, and graphics – analytical tools that group members find intuitive, memorable, agreeable, and ultimately "actionable."[1]

---

[1] A "framework" is a lens, mental model, or analytical tool, often represented in a graphic, set of principles, story, or agreement. It is a tool or device that helps us interpret what is or was happening (how things are or were), explore how things could or should be, and decide how best to apply ourselves. Frameworks get at the structure of situations and solutions.

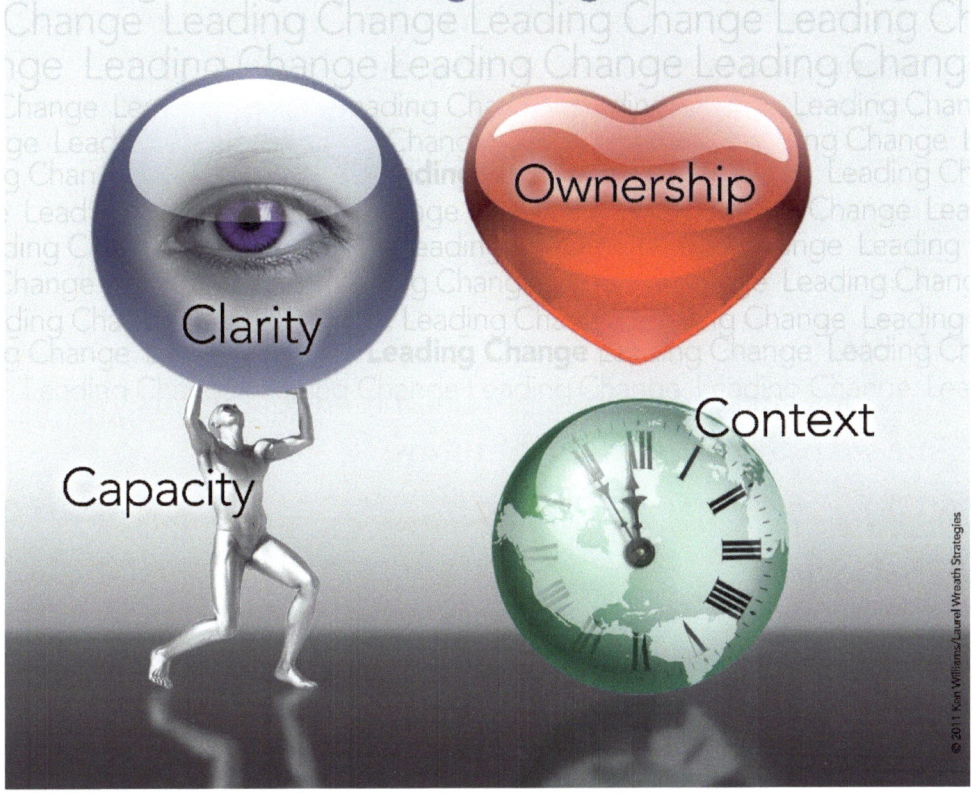

Foundations of Practice

The work of a visionary group is a journey together. This quest for impact can begin with and return habitually to a set of questions members of the group find helpful to consider as they engage with stakeholders[2] in the endeavor. Here are sample questions a group may regularly entertain.

Clarity

What does success look like to us in concrete terms? What is our shared vision of a great future?

What are our primary strategies to get to this "place" of shared victory?

What are the sequences we should follow as we apply our time, energy, and resources?

What will be the signs or indicators ("milestones") that show we are making progress?

Are there activities or investments for which we need to review our intentions or motivations, i.e., our purposes?

---

[2] A "stakeholder" is someone who has something to gain or lose if an endeavor is successful or unsuccessful. Typically, a stakeholder also brings special capabilities or valuable perspective to the effort.

Notes:

Context

What are recent developments in the world, our field of work, community, network, or institution – the factors that should influence decision making? What breaking news is relevant?

What *trends* may accelerate, impede, or otherwise affect our progress?

What does our "information pipeline" look like? Who are the sources of information, the "curators," we presently trust and rely upon for valuable content?

How are we "plugged in" to repositories and flows of data? Is it time to open up new channels? Are there people or organizations we should engage? Are there subscriptions (paper or electronic) we should purchase?

Are there networks we should join for the sake of staying current?

What else can we do to stay attuned to relevant contexts for our work?

Is there also "weeding out" we need to conduct because we are overwhelmed by *too much* information?

Notes:

Capacity

What capabilities do we need to develop or enhance to achieve our vision of success? What resources do we need to secure?

How might we map our current and desired capabilities?

What are the systems and processes we need to establish or refine to manage capacity efficiently? Where is there waste in the current system?

Where are there unseen talents that can be deployed?

What networks can be tapped to draw new capacity to the effort?

To whom should we turn for valuable support?

How are we building capabilities among our members and instituting policies and practices that will enable us to remain sustainable over time?

Given our present limitations, are there other groups better suited to lead some component of this work?

How can culture serve not only as a context for our work, but also as a resource to us?

Notes:

Ownership

How is this work meaningful and fulfilling to us? Are we truly enthusiastic about this work? What would help us get more excited about this endeavor? What needs to change to unleash our passion and sustain our energy?

Are we satisfied with what we're receiving from this work?

Are our role definitions clear, flexible, and appropriate?

How is influence exercised in this system? Does everyone have a voice?

Is creative input habitually invited and welcomed? Is candid feedback appreciated even if it challenges the status quo?

Are important decisions arrived at through consensus to every extent possible? Where is there a sense of alienation or frustration in the enterprise, and how should we address it?

How might we best recognize or reward creativity and sacrifice? How can we honor each person's contributions? What deserves to be celebrated?

Notes:

Further Analysis

The questions under each of the four headings above are merely illustrative and can be freely drawn from or adapted. It is unlikely that a group would utilize all of them. In addition, the choice of question format depends on context. There are times when it makes sense to frame a question in a binary (yes/no) format. In other cases, it makes sense to pose the question in an open-ended format (i.e., who, what, when, where, how, and why).

It is important not to use the format of a question as a means to skirt uncomfortable conversations as sometimes happens. Group members should be free to discuss and reframe the questions throughout the exchange.

The four-part framework represented above (context, clarity, capacity, and ownership) is one of many tools facilitative leaders can deploy to focus group time and energy. A group can *habitually* return to such a framework to share status, structure focus, and make critical decisions.

Notes:

Focusing Attention, Confirming Intentions

A facilitative approach to leadership involves giving encouragement and issuing challenges to stakeholders as group focus shifts over time. At one point, people are exchanging status updates. "What is going on?" "What is happening?" At another point, the group is resetting direction and adjusting strategy. "What is our plan?" "What are our next steps?" "Where do we go from here?" The bulk of a group's time together is spent on information sharing, decision making, and collective action.

In addition to supporting group focus, the facilitative leader strives to protect and promote candor among stakeholders. Members should feel safe to raise questions such as "Why are we doing this?" "What are our intentions?" "What is motivating us?" Thus the mature and responsible group is not threatened by shifts between 1) the fine-tuning of direction and strategy and 2) the acknowledgement of aims and purposes.

The creative process of supporting a group's focus is analogous to a common exercise we go through in the course of the standard eye exam. The optometrist asks us to close one eye and then the other to determine whether there are issues with our vision and whether a prescription or surgery may be necessary. A facilitative leader supports a group in utilizing appropriate "lenses" for situation analysis and consensus building.

Focused Leadership

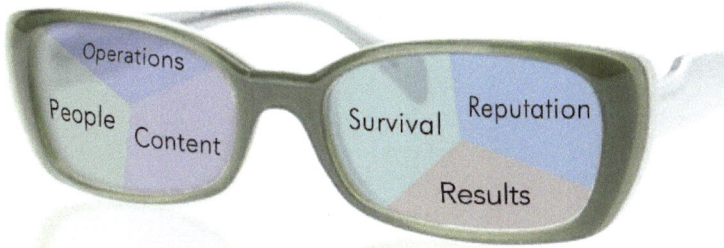

Content, People, Operations

Content

Within a facilitative process, a group can focus analysis and decision making on the substance of its work. Substance or work "content" may include products, services, projects, programs, subjects, and fields.

People

A group can discuss relationship development and progress made in engaging stakeholders. Members may explore how people currently participate and how people could contribute to an initiative. The group considers the roles, rights, responsibilities, and accomplishments of influential participants. Every enterprise can gain from having a "people strategy."

Operations

Finally, a group can identify or return to a set of operational considerations — systems and processes, budgetary requirements, infrastructure, and material conditions that undergird the entire initiative.

Survival, Reputation, Results

Survival

A group can explicitly acknowledge what its members are doing or must do simply to assure survival. What do we do to keep the lights on? What assures that the doors stay open? Where is there a sense of urgency at present?

Reputation

A group can discuss what people are doing or need to do for the sake of reputation or brand development. How much weight do we give to what others think of us? What are people saying about us? What are we doing primarily to make a good impression on others? How can we measure confidence in and respect for our work? How can we tell our story better? What counts as promotion or marketing? Should we invest more in strategic communications?

Results

Finally, a group can take note of what people are doing or must do in order to deliver tangible impacts, to satisfy stakeholder expectations. What can people reasonably expect from us? What progress are we making towards our vision of success? What are the milestones we have attained? How are we delivering on the promise of our enterprise? What do we have to celebrate?

Notes:

Nurturing Trust

Trust is a critical asset for groups striving to attain both focus and impact. Trust enables people to draw on each other's capabilities and to build on each other's contributions. Trust unleashes energy and fosters agility. Trust is a special form of power.

It's been said that we live in a knowledge economy. However, the market value of knowledge is often short-lived due to the proliferation of free content on the internet. Perhaps it is more accurate to say that we live in a "trust economy." Knowledge may contribute to trust, but knowledge is often not enough to anchor powerful collaborations.

A good way to explore the level and quality of trust that people place in a group or the trust that members have among themselves is to apply a framework such as the one represented in the graphic on the next page. This framework can help to focus efforts to *build* trust as well as efforts to *repair* trust when it has broken down.

Confidentiality

Gossip is often harmful. Trust can be destroyed by the release of personal or proprietary information. Trust suffers when embargoes or nondisclosure agreements are violated. It is difficult to move an agenda forward when members of a group share information inappropriately. It is also difficult to succeed when members feel it is unsafe to share information. In some organizations and communities, there are individuals highly regarded for their ability to keep secrets and honor privacy. Sometimes breaches in expected confidentiality can actually help to *build trust* in the integrity of a group, as in the case of whistle blowing. *Facilitator's question*s: Are there specific issues with confidentiality that need to be acknowledged and addressed in this endeavor? If so, how?

Candor

A culture of candor can be a tremendous asset to a group. Appreciation and support for honesty enables decisions to be based on the true value of each person's perspective or understanding. A sense of collegiality, community, or solidarity grows when sincerity serves as a starting point. People feel that they have greater integrity when "what you see is what you get" and all is "above board." Groups suffer trauma from bait-and-switch approaches or the discovery of hidden motives. Organizations demonstrate a commitment to institutional honesty when they introduce policies and practices that reflect transparency. *Facilitator's questions:* Are there specific issues with candor, honesty, or transparency in this endeavor that need to be acknowledged and addressed? If so, how?

Perceived Capacity

Funders, donors, and investors usually size up a group or company before writing a check. They want to know that the necessary infrastructure, systems, and people are in place to assure success. They want to know that the leaders of an initiative have the requisite knowledge and skills or can develop such capabilities within an appropriate timeframe. Members of a particular group may also size up one another. They may take note of factors such as money, experience, position, credentials, perceived intelligence, and level of energy available for collective work. Reservoirs of capacity can create hope. Gaps in capacity can create doubt. *Facilitator's questions:* Are there specific issues related to perceived capacity of our group that need to be acknowledged and addressed? If so, how?

Observed Performance

People tend to trust leaders or groups they have seen deliver on promises. A group can be undermined when it fails to keep commitments and even fracture or dissolve when a member does not pull his weight or fulfill his responsibilities. Indicators that may be pertinent include the pace and timeliness of work; efficiency and agility; volume of output; quality control and evidence of passion for excellence; group harmony; and ethics and integrity. For some observers, seeing outstanding performance contributes to believing in future possibilities. Facilitator's questions: Are there specific issues related to performance that need to be acknowledged and addressed in order to build or restore trust? If so, how?

Testimonial

Strong testimonials and a solid reputation can lead to unexpected opportunities for a group. Accolades and awards can factor into a person's career advancement and further entrustment with authority and control over resources. A former client's or customer's words can open doors to new collaborations. People seek out referrals and recommendations. By way of contrast, criticism can severely damage the reputation of an institution or leader. Bad reviews can sink a product. Testimonials are assets that can be deployed to build or restore trust. *Facilitator's questions:* Are there specific issues related to our reputation or brand we need to acknowledge and address? If so, how? What are people saying about us?

Notes:

Transforming Conflict

Conflict is inevitable in ambitious endeavors that strain the capabilities and test the patience of group members. How can the facilitative leader or the group that shares facilitation manage tension, disagreement, or outright hostility?

The first step is to secure recognition or admission among the involved parties that there is a conflict, that conflict is inevitable, and that a conflict is presently interfering with or could interfere with the attainment of major milestones of importance to stakeholders.

The second step is to get at the source of the conflict. Is this conflict due to prior history among the parties involved? Is it due to specific incidents? Is there disagreement about the mission, the vision, or the objectives of the overall endeavor? Do the parties have diverging views about what success looks like? Or is the disagreement not so much about ends as it is about means, how to bring about the vision through strategies and tactics? Is there a fight over resources? Does the conflict have to do with who is getting credit or recognition? Are there problems with role definitions and expectations? Is the tension due simply to differences in tastes, aesthetics, or personal preferences?

The third step in the process of facilitating transformation of conflict is to secure agreement as to what approach or method would be most effective in resolving the issues at hand. Would a dialogue aimed at consensus or compromise be sufficient? Would it be prudent to engage a qualified mediator? Would the groups accept the outcome of a binding arbitration in which responsibility for a solution has been entrusted with a reasonable, mutually acceptable party? Would spending time together in a natural setting away from hustle and bustle be conducive to less tense, more productive conversations? Is there a cultural asset — a tradition, symbol, ritual, work of art, or protocol for healing – that can be introduced to help address problems at hand or to root out hostility and instill understanding and empathy?

The fourth step is to brainstorm a list of attributes or qualities that help to define a perfect or acceptable solution. These markers might include attainment of specific milestones, approval of the solution by specified stakeholders, a redefinition of roles, the redistribution of resources, protection of reputations, creating new opportunities, and sharing fruits of collaboration. Assuring that the parties in conflict secure a full and fair hearing is also critical.

The fifth step in managing conflict is to develop a plan for implementation of the solution. This includes monitoring compliance with the agreement, managing and processing emotions, and troubleshooting. Group attentiveness helps to assure that the conflict does not "rear its ugly head again" or crop up in some other form. If the conflict is not sufficiently resolved, the involved parties must decide whether they will continue to work toward a solution, postpone further discussion, conduct one or more pilot tests, or acknowledge that the group will have to recompose itself or disband altogether.

As the group strives to bring about consensus, compromise, or reconciliation among the parties in conflict, a facilitative leader monitors and addresses the dynamics of civility and incivility, helps the group identify opportunities for creativity and experimentation, draws attention to shared benefits and the need for reciprocity, and interjects humor whenever appropriate and conducive to moving forward.

Notes:

Conclusion

Facilitative approaches to leadership rely on humility, openness, and positive regard for one another. A facilitative leader supports a group as it becomes attuned to its evolving context, seeks clarity of purpose and strategy, addresses capacity gaps, and shares ownership in what will hopefully turn out to be a successful endeavor.

Facilitative leaders assist groups in achieving focus on the substantial, personal, and operational aspects of work. They create space for confirming group intentions as energy and resources are expended for the sake of survival, reputation development, and positive contributions to society.

Facilitative leaders also build and restore trust among stakeholders. This trust is buoyed by regard for confidentiality, transparency, capacity formation, commitment to excellence, and positive testimonials.

Facilitative leaders strive to resolve the conflicts that impair progress. They help rekindle passion among caring individuals and utilize processes that stimulate regeneration within institutions and communities. The practice of facilitative leadership establishes conditions essential to the formation of bonds among persons and organizations.

Facilitative leadership is rooted in the values of equality, fairness and human dignity. Such leadership relies on full confidence that every stakeholder has something of significant value to contribute.

Surely the time has come for commitments throughout the world to the exercise of leadership as the honorable practice of agile, creative, appreciative facilitation.

Further Reading

Bass, Bernard M., and Ronald E. Riggio. *Transformational Leadership*. 2nd ed. Mahwah: Lawrence Erlbaum Associates, Inc., 2006, 282 pages.

Gardiner, John. *On Leadership*. New York: The Free Press, 1993, 220 pages.

Goethals, George R., and Georgia L. J. Sorenson, eds. *The Quest for a General Theory of Leadership*. Northampton, MA: Edward Elgar Publishing, 2006, 250 pages.

Goleman, D., R. Boyatzis, and A. McKee. *Primal Leadership: Realizing the Power of Emotional Intelligence*. Boston: Harvard Business School Press, 2002, 306 pages.

Lipman-Blumen, Jean. *Connective Leadership: Managing in a Changing World*. Oxford: Oxford University Press, 1996, 407 pages.

Heifetz, Ronald. *Leadership on the Line: Staying Alive through the Dangers of Leading*. Boston: Harvard Business School Press, 2002, 252 pages.

Kouzes, James M., and Barry Z. Posner. *The Leadership Challenge*. 4th ed. San Francisco: Jossey-Bass Publishers, 2007, 392 pages.

Napolitano, Carole S., and Lida J. Henderson. *The Leadership Odyssey: A Self-Development Guide to*

New Skills for New Times. San Francisco: Jossey-Bass Publishers, 1998, 271 pages.

Northouse, Peter G. *Introduction to Leadership Concepts and Practices*. 2nd ed. Thousand Oaks, CA: Sage Publications, 2012, 274 pages.

Northouse, Peter G. *Leadership: Theory and Practice*. Thousand Oaks, CA: Sage Publications, 2004, 344 pages.

Williams, Ken. *A Future of Leadership Development*. AED Center for Leadership Development, 2009, 23 pages.

Web Sites

Alliance for Nonprofit Management
 www.allianceonline.org

American Management Association
www.amanet.org

American Society for Training and Development
www.astd.org

American Society of Association Executives
www.asaecenter.org

Board Source
www.boardsource.org

Center for Creative Leadership
www.ccl.org

Center for Nonprofit Advancement
www.nonprofitadvancement.org

International Coach Federation
www.coachfederation.org

International Leadership Association
www.ila-net.org

Leadership Learning Community
www.leadershiplearning.org

Leadership for a Changing World
www.leadershipforchange.org

Linkage Incorporated
www.linkageinc.com

Jossey-Bass Publishing
www.josseybass.com

Dedication

To my family, friends, and the New Voices Community

Acknowledgements

Graphic Design: Jeff Williams, Parallax Studio

Layout and Copy Editing: Matthew Testa

Author's Contact information

Ken Todd Williams
contactktw@gmail.com
www.winksite.com/KenTodd/Williams